If you made it this far, a big thanks to you!

I hope you liked it.

One more disclaimer: While this book is kind of fictitious, still, any resemblance between characters and events in this book and real people and events is purely coincidental.

And now for my second shameless plug!

Hopefully within the next year, my first actual original book.

Quinsigamond Saves The Day!

Check out

Quinsigamondsavestheday.com

for more information.

And in the end, SHE WINS!

Of course, she does.

Yes, that is a Dalek. Why do you ask?

Has there ever been in the history of mattress sales, a mattress sale that wasn't a **giant** mattress sale?

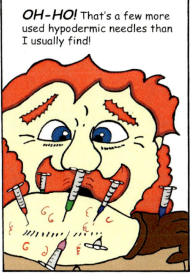

Even our relatively Urb-burbish neighborhood, Noe Valley, isn't immune to the opioid epidemic. I met one of the gardeners and she showed me the needles in one of the planters. She wondered why the addicts couldn't be more careful about where they put their used needles. Then she added neatness probably isn't high on their list of priorities. That's why they're addicts.

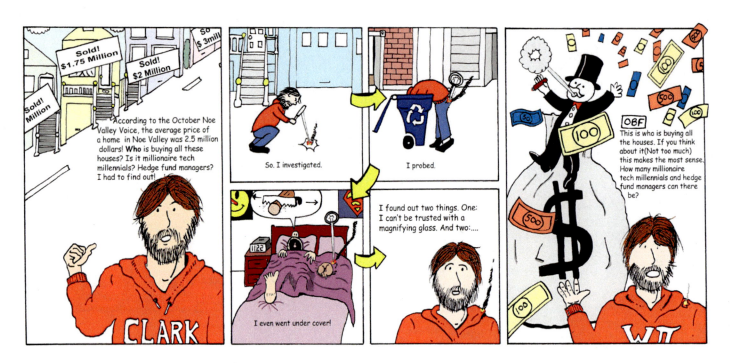

A San Francisco Safeway worker just won two million dollars in the state lottery. He said he was hoping to buy a house. He only thinks he can buy a house in San Francisco for two million dollars.

Ovis knew, he just HAD to level up his game

This is the third mountain goat cartoon I've done in my life and the second one in this book. The first one I did was in my first cartoon book, "Owen Baker-Flynn in Black and White and a Little Red All Over." That book is hopelessly out of print, but you can still get it through Blurb.com at:

http://www.blurb.com/b/5539157-owen-baker-flynn-in-black-and-white-and-a-little-r

How's that for a shameless plug, eh? And I guess the fact that you can still get it means it's not "hopelessly out of print."

Ever since the Noe Valley Voice said I could add color to the cartoons I'd been trying to figure out a way to do a cartoon that would start in pencil and work towards a color end. I ended up doing the opposite in this particular cartoon, but I like the way this turned out.

Poor Sue Grafton! That was harsh! A through Y? That was so sad!

The thing I really liked about her books was that the stories got better and she got better too.

Grobf was an early proponent of the, "Paleoreo Diet."

I actually wouldn't be surprised if San Francisco did this, which is pretty telling. I mean I really like it here, but sometimes I think the people running things look out the window and go, "WaitaMINUTE! People and cars are getting where they need to go...well we'd better put a stop to that!" I ride my bike about 30 miles a week and **I** think they've gone overboard with the bike lanes, especially the Market Street Slalom Bike Lane of Death! You're on the right! You're in the middle of the street! Then back on the right! Back to the middle! All the while cars and trucks are also doing that same thing. By the way, I really do ride my bike that much. And the hills? Yup, I go up those hills. (I'm not winning races or anything.) If you're going to ride your bike in San Francisco you have to embrace the hills. But, if you pay attention to the topography, you can avoid going any higher than necessary.

I have an unbelievably small business which I conduct out of my apartment. I have a business license and a resale permit. My federal and state tax returns are each about 25 pages long. I can't imagine what a pain it must be for a small corner store that has to track each bag of potato chips. I think the thing that gets me the most is that there are all these rules teeny businesses have to follow while we're making it easier for coal and chemical companies to dump their wastes in our waters.

"Biff! Get the right box!"

Out on Treasure Island, in the middle of San Francisco Bay, there used to be a store just as you drove onto the island; it looked very similar to the one in this cartoon, and that store had both of those signs on the side of the building. I always imagined someone getting confused about what they were buying. Also, the on-ramp from Treasure Island onto westbound Interstate 80 on the Bay Bridge is, I believe, one of the few on-ramps to an interstate highway that has a stop sign right before you get on the Interstate Highway. So, getting on the Bay Bridge is basically 0 to 50 MPH in..............NOW!

Shot with an iPhone 6 Semiautomatic

Several iPhones ago, Apple had billboards all over town with really nice photos and the caption,

"Shot with an iPhone 6S." I just added a little more to it.

My wife was hit by a car a few years ago, so this cartoon was my public way of saying thank you to those that helped her.

Also, I think it's kind of funny that we may live upstairs from Dagwood Bumstead.

Olwynn Takes an "Elfie!"

"I don't know Santa, maybe you shoulda parked on the roof!

In the criminal justice system, the people are represented by two separate and equally important groups: The police who investigate crime, and the district attorney who prosecutes those offenders. **Unless!** Your car (or sled) is broken into in San Francisco. Then... you're on your own, kid! I tell you this not to scare you, but to encourage you not to leave stuff in your car. So, if you're going to San Francisco, wear flowers in your hair, and DO NOT leave stuff in your car. Or sled.

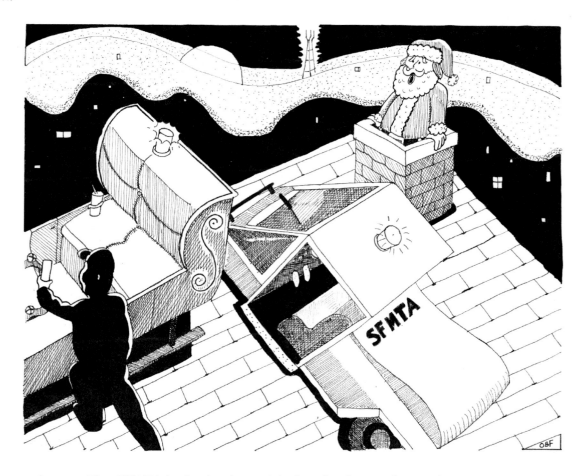

The SFMTA is absolutely, positively relentless in their ticket issuing.
(Even if your vehicle has been stolen!)

And that's how he does it all in one night! The Dasher App! Now available on iTunes, Google Play, and Just For Fun!

Just For Fun is a store in Noe Valley and they always have neat stuff. Over the years I've done a number of cartoons that suggested you could buy things that don't really exist at their store. Either they have a great sense of humor, or they've never seen the cartoons, because I've never gotten a complaint from them.

This appeared in a Spring 2018 Noe Valley Voice. I had just read that people in Paris rioted over the price of Nutella. Now, I like Nutella as much as the next guy, as long as the next guy isn't Parisian I guess, but it still didn't make much sense. And of course, we in Noe Valley would never…. well maybe we would.

And now, for some Santa Claus cartoons…

They're back!

Came networking through wireless wood

And quickened as he came.

1,2! 1,2! I'm a PC!

The Power Point did an easy hack

He left it dead and Defender

And zuned his service pack.

And hast thou slain the MacBook Pro?

Oh my, my Defragmenter boy!

O Windows! O Groove! Hip-Hooray!

He Outlooked in his joy.

Twas Vista and the Auto Collage

Did XP and Word in the RAM

All Free Cell were the Gwabbitage...

This Poem has performed an illegal operation. Press OK to continue

Twas Vista and Auto Collage   Did XP and...File not found!

The Jabbertechie!

T'was Vista and the autocollage

Did XP and Word in the RAM.

All Free Cell were the Gwabbitage

And the works CD ROM.

Beware the MacBook Pro my son

Its OS, its Bytes, the Air Port.

Beware the quick Quicktime and shun

The Polycarbonate iPod!

He took his Powerpoint in hand,

Long time the SQL server he sought

So, confirmed? He by the Xbox land

And scheduled tasks in thought.

And as in Office Suite he stood

The MacBook Pro, optics aflame

THAT'S *MISTER* Coffee TO YOU!

And now, a text break. Introducing...

And while I'm on the subject of umpires...

When congressional lobbyists become Little League parents.

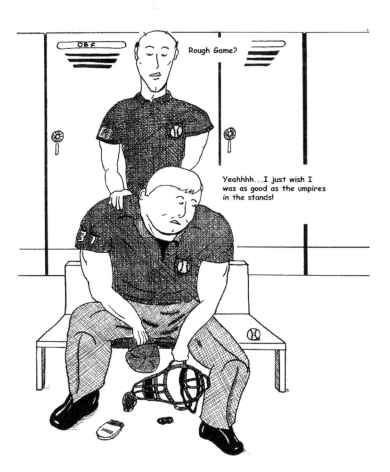

I've been umpiring High School baseball for about 9 years. I'm kind of good at it, not the best, but most of the time okay. Every now and then there's a loud mouth parent who thinks he or she can do a better job than me and lets me know that fact. I often suggest to them we're hiring. Not one of those parents has applied yet.

Maybe it's the semi-evil influence of Jasper Fforde or <u>Who Framed Roger Rabbit</u> but I've always liked the idea that maybe there's a world behind the comic strip; that maybe the characters from all the strips know each other, hang out, that there's some sort of infrastructure, whatever. Also, any similarity between the two construction workers in this cartoon and Laurel and Hardy means I'm a better artist than I thought.

Two construction workers broke an undercartoon ink main today. Ink cleanup will take about four weeks. The Animal Company has offered to clean any animal affected by the ink main break for free. Remember! Always check under cartoons before digging!

If you're unfamiliar with Jasper Fforde start with <u>The Eyre Affair</u>.

If you're unfamiliar with <u>Who Framed Roger Rabbit</u>, see it. The story and effects hold up really well 30 years later.

We have an early earthquake warning system in our apartment. My wife has a kitchen wall filled with cake pans of all different shapes and sizes. On August 24, 2014, the night of the Napa Earthquake, right before the house started shaking like crazy, all those cake pans started vibrating and humming. You could hear them and by the time I figured out what that weird noise was, the house started shaking like crazy.

So now I know, if the cake pans are hummin', a quake's a comin'!

9/15/17 After exploring the solar system for 20 years Cassini plunges into Saturn and burns up in Saturn's atmosphere.

9/16/17 Cassini returns to Earth with a note taped on the side. In English. Somehow.

I even more rarely do two topical cartoons on the same subject.

I rarely do topical humor in cartoons, but I was so impressed with space probe Cassini. After 20 years exploring space we crashed Cassini into Saturn. I wondered how the Saturnalians felt about that.

*I **knowww** crows are smart, Bob! But come on! Partner smart?*

I submitted this cartoon to the New Yorker. I thought they might go for it as it seems very "New Yorkery." They didn't, but the upside is, if they had, you would've had to pay a lot more for this book.

That book will have "As Seen in The New Yorker" in big letters on the cover.

Nancy's Tailors was a real place at 701 Leavenworth Street in San Francisco. Leavenworth Street is probably not as steep as it's portrayed here. The funny thing to me is that the "Alteration s" sign with the "s" on its own line was the actual sign in the window. I always wondered who would have their clothes altered at a place that couldn't make "Alterations" fit on one line? You'd just be asking to have one pant leg longer than the other.

They didn't think the idea was as good or as funny as I thought it was, but they did print the actual cartoon.

Also, if you look carefully, the margins are being seriously disrespected here. Often, I look at margins as a suggestion, sometimes to be taken seriously, and sometimes to be ignored.

A near total eclipse passed over San Francisco in August of 2017. I asked the Noe Valley Voice to consider publishing two cartoons in their September issue. (Two! Two for the price of one, or BOGO as the kids say.) I thought it could be funny to think about an eclipse passing over as I was drawing the cartoon. And then they could print the actual cartoon a couple of pages later.

MORTIMER WAS ALWAYS A LITTLE..... UNCONVENTIONAL

This cartoon was rejected by the New Yorker. Sometimes I submit thinking this'll never fly, but I did think this one might get past the gatekeeper. >sigh< Someday.

There really is a Garden of the Humanitarians in Golden Gate Park.

Full Disclosure: It doesn't really have giant planter pots with actual humanitarians growing in them.

Ovis was right! His rival wasn't expecting nun-chuks!

This is the second cartoon I've done featuring mountain goats. That's a pretty big number considering I have very little experience with mountain goats.

As we will continue to see, it's a mystery to me what this woman sees in this guy and why she stays with him.

She must really like him or something.

ABSO-FREAKIN'-LUTELY! YOU WANT YOUR BOSS DEAD AND YOU WANT IT
TO LOOK LIKE YOUR MUDDER-IN-LAW DID IT! WE CAN MAKE THAT HAPPEN!

This is a newer cartoon. All shaded with Photoshop. I did hand draw the Custom Framing sign, mainly because I couldn't figure out how to reverse the text in Photoshop. >sigh!< Someday.

This may be the oldest cartoon in the book, it's certainly old enough to recall the days of VHS tape!

It's also old enough that I used to actually write the text in the cartoon. My handwriting has deteriorated so much over the years I could write right or left handed and you couldn't tell the difference. In that respect, I'm ambidextrous!

Noe Valley is the home of the Two Million Dollar Home. It's been a while since anything went for less. Even a fixer upper recently went for a million dollars. So, it was a big surprise to many of us when a crystal meth lab was discovered and busted in this hood. We thought that sort of thing was reserved for RVs and Albuquerque, New Mexico. And yeah, I'm a big fan of Breaking Bad.

I've started using color in my cartoons, but I'm glad I didn't use color for this one.

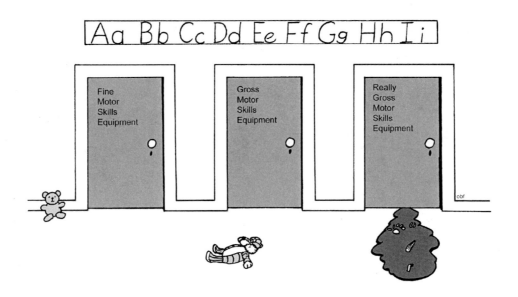

And speaking of color...

This was first published in the Noe Valley Voice, probably the fall of 2015. The SFMTA, the people in charge of buses, trains, and causing traffic in San Francisco "fixed" the San Jose Avenue off ramp, which is a MILE long. When they were done, traffic was often backed up the entire mile and then on to Interstate 280. They called it a success. Before their handiwork, traffic could actually move. I have another cartoon on the SFMTA mission which seems to be to make sure no one can get anywhere, but I'll space them out so I don't come off as a total crank.

Now lissen up! This is where the hoo-mans keep their best food! Trust me...you'll know it when you see it!

I'll return to this theme a few times before this book is done. I think half the people you see

at Bay Area Starbucks (Starbuck's? Starbuckses? I have no idea!) are working on new killer apps.

Second Dedication

This book is also dedicated to every single public school teacher I ever had, including the ones who drove me nuts and the ones I drove nuts, starting with Mrs. Warner in Kindergarten at PS 8 in the Bronx. After that, the ones I can remember, though I might have the spelling or the Miss/Mrs, wrong: Mr. Keleher, Mrs. Ulmer, Mrs. Crawford, Mr. Noel, Mr. Vermette, Mr. Allen, Mrs. Macksoud, Mr. Lowery, Mr. Brayton, Mr. Leblond, Mr. Barone, Mr. Dulude, Mr. Antunes, Mrs. Wentworth, Miss Nashuawaty, Mrs. Harrower, Mr. Goss, Miss Pacheco, Mr. Cunningham, Miss Dye, Miss McCann, Mr. Minnicuci, Mr. Carlos, Mr. Bianchi, etc. I've probably missed one or two. (Hey! It's been over 40 years, cut me some slack.) Every one of those teachers worked tirelessly to get something through this thick skull of mine, while at the same time I resisted many of their efforts. If you like this book, and I hope you do, it's in large part because of all the teachers I've had in my life who showed me something, taught me something, or took time out of their day for some extra help.

(If you didn't like this book, well that's totally on me!)

More thanks. #thisisgettinglikeanoscaracceptancespeech

Thanks to David Amaral and Peter Fournier for the assist on teachers' names.

Thanks to Terry Sherman for a big save on a misspelled name and thanks to Sara Baker-Flynn for proofreading this one more time..

Thanks to Stan Zompakos. There couldn't be a better friend.

And finally, apologies to Lewis Carroll

My Second Book of Cartoons!

By owen baker-flynn

This book is dedicated to my wife Laurie. Without her everything would be a lot harder. It's also dedicated to my kids, Dylan and Sara. Thanks to me, they have perfected their, "Ooh nice. Must not roll my eyes right now" look.

Now for a little bit of business.

ISBN #: 13: 978-0-578-49967-3

And for librarians: 1. American wit and humor, pictoral

Thanks to the Noe Valley Voice for publishing many of these cartoons and special thanks to Noe Valley Voice editor Sally Smith! Who knew commas could be so hard? Well, she does!

And thanks to the Marin County Fair for a fair number of awards for these cartoons.